*This book was purchased
with funds from a
generous donation by*

Dr. Kathryn W. Davis

CALIFORNIA
MISSIONS

Discovering Mission San Buenaventura

BY SAM HAMILTON

1782

Cavendish Square
New York

Published in 2015 by Cavendish Square Publishing, LLC
243 5th Avenue, Suite 136, New York, NY 10016

Website: cavendishsq.com

This publication represents the opinions and views of the author based on his or her personal experience, knowledge, and research. The information in this book serves as a general guide only. The author and publisher have used their best efforts in preparing this book and disclaim liability rising directly or indirectly from the use and application of this book.

CPSIA Compliance Information: Batch #WS14CSQ

All websites were available and accurate when this book was sent to press.

Library of Congress Cataloging-in-Publication Data

Hamilton, Sam.
Discovering Mission San Buenaventura / Sam Hamilton.
pages cm — (California missions)
Includes index.
ISBN 978-1-62713-103-2 (hardcover) ISBN 978-1-62713-105-6 (ebook)
1. San Buenaventura Mission—History—Juvenile works. 2. Franciscans—California—Ventura—History—Juvenile works. 3. Chumash Indians—Missions—California—Ventura—History—Juvenile works. 4. Spanish mission buildings—California—Ventura—History—Juvenile works. 5. California—History—To 1846—Juvenile works. I. Title.
F869.S187H35 2015
979.4'92—dc 3
2014008346

Editorial Director: Dean Miller
Editor: Kristen Susienka
Copy Editor: Cynthia Roby
Art Director: Jeffrey Talbot
Designer: Douglas Brooks
Photo Researcher: J8 Media
Production Manager: Jennifer Ryder-Talbot
Production Editor: David McNamara

Printed in the United States of America

CALIFORNIA
MISSIONS

Contents

Mission San Buenaventura is a lasting memento of a transformative part of California's early history.

1
Spanish Explorers in California

Along California's coast, from San Diego to Sonoma, a chain of missions stand as reminders of some of the most eventful moments in the state's history. Part of this landscape is Mission San Buenaventura, which has been around for more than 200 years.

In 1493, Christopher Columbus brought back news of the New World (the areas we now know as South America, Central America, and North America) to Spain. Many Europeans consequently went to the New World hoping to find gold, or a river that could take them through the continent, connecting the Atlantic and Pacific Oceans. They believed that this would provide a faster way to get to Asia, where they could buy silks and spices to sell at home.

In the 1520s and 1530s, Spanish explorers and soldiers like Hernán Cortés and Francisco Pizarro conquered the great civilizations of the Aztecs and Incas in the lands that are now Mexico and Peru. When Cortés conquered the area that is now Mexico, the Spanish named this area **New Spain**. By expanding from New Spain into other areas of North America, Spain hoped to grow even larger and wealthier.

Cabrillo is remembered as one of the first Spanish explorers to navigate the coast of California.

EXPLORING NEW SPAIN

Juan Rodríguez Cabrillo first visited the western coast of North America in 1542. He and the crew of his ship, the *San Salvador*, sailed from New Spain, up the coast of *Baja*, or "lower," California, and into *Alta*, or "upper," California, and claimed these coastal lands for Spain.

Cabrillo and his men found their first port on September 28, 1542, in what is now San Diego Bay. He and his crew continued sailing north, and in the first half of October, the expedition reached San Pedro, Santa Monica, San Buenaventura, Santa Barbara, and Point Concepción.

Cabrillo died in January 1543, midway through the voyage. After his death, Cabrillo's crew continued to sail as far north as the area that is now the state of Oregon. They proved that Alta California was not an island, as some had thought, but was instead part of a large mainland.

The rulers of Spain, however, still wanted to find a trade route connecting the Atlantic and Pacific Oceans. When explorers failed to find such a route, the Spanish government decided to stop funding these voyages. After a failed attempt by explorer Sebastián Vizcaíno in 1602, no Spanish ships sailed to Alta California for the next 160 years.

2
The Chumash People

In the area that spans what is now Malibu to San Luis Obispo, the Spanish encountered the *Chumash*. They called themselves "The First People," and were one of the most prosperous of the California tribes.

This prosperity was increased by their skill on the sea. This skill was developed by very few of the California tribes, as the majority of the **indigenous people** would move inland from season to season in search of available food in the wild instead of looking to the oceans, which could be rough and dangerous. The Chumash were known for building *tomols*, boats that were quick and strong, which were used to fish, trade, and travel to places such as the Channel Islands. Constructed to hold up to ten people, tomols were made out of planks of wood. Holes were drilled in the planks, which were fastened with rope made of plant fibers and by a glue made out of pine sap and natural tar.

The Chumash were expert boat makers and crafted large vessels to fish and hunt marine life for food.

ARTISANS AND ARTISTS

Nature provided the Chumash people with plenty of food, so there was no need to farm. Instead, the Chumash men fished and hunted for small animals, while the women gathered fruits, nuts, and vegetables. The Chumash women also wove beautiful baskets, which were so well made that they were waterproof when the insides were coated with tar. These baskets were in demand long after the mission period, and the Chumash produced them until the last weavers died around 1915.

The Chumash also made intricate baskets, some of which could carry water.

The Chumash were artistic in other ways. They have left behind colorful cave art and **petroglyphs** that are now protected by the National Park System, and studied by historians, anthropologists, and archaeologists from all over the world.

Before the arrival of the Spanish explorers, soldiers, and **missionaries**, the Chumash lived in 150 villages spread over approximately 7,000 square miles (11,265 kilometers). Each village was led by a chief, while a shaman acted as the tribe's spiritual leader. The chief was in charge of passing out food and valuables to the tribe members. He or she would also lead their villagers into

Each Native tribe had traditional Native dress that they wore when celebrating special occasions.

war. The biggest disputes were usually over land. The shaman was the religious leader, giving advice and helping cure the sick. The shaman performed rituals believed to bring rain. While men usually served in the chief and shaman positions, women sometimes held these roles as well.

Every village had at least one *temescal*, or sweat lodge. These lodges were used by men before religious ceremonies or hunting trips. After sweating in front of a fire, the men would bathe in cool water. This process was believed to cure illnesses and provide other benefits to the body, mind, and spirit.

PASTIMES

The Chumash also built playing fields, called *malamtepupi*, which were level, smooth, and walled. It was here that they

The Salinan, Chumash, and Yokut are known today for their pictographs, drawn on the walls of caves.

played games such hoop and pole, in which a spear or an arrow was propelled through a rolling hoop that was four or five inches (10 to 12 centimeters) in diameter. *Shinny,* or *tikauwich,* a form of field hockey, was also popular. The villagers placed bets on the outcome of these games, and they also gambled with games using dice.

Chumash houses were dome-shaped and made out of wood and reeds. They could hold as many as fifty people. To make a house, the Chumash shaped wood into thin poles, which they bent into a rounded roof and reinforced with whalebone. Then the structures were covered with *tule,* reeds that were woven tightly. Entire tribes would work together to construct and maintain their homes, creating a community of shared responsibility and respect.

3
The
Mission System

When Russian and English explorers reached the western coast of North America, Spain became concerned that it would lose the land that Cabrillo and Vizcaíno had claimed. The Spanish quickly took measures to permanently control the California land.

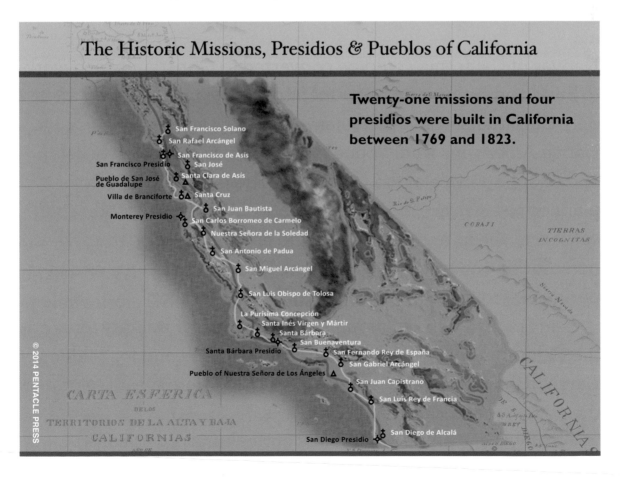

The Historic Missions, Presidios & Pueblos of California

Twenty-one missions and four presidios were built in California between 1769 and 1823.

San Francisco Solano
San Rafael Arcángel
San Francisco de Asís
San Francisco Presidio
San José
Pueblo de San José de Guadalupe
Santa Clara de Asis
Villa de Branciforte
Santa Cruz
San Juan Bautista
Monterey Presidio
San Carlos Borromeo de Carmelo
Nuestra Señora de la Soledad
San Antonio de Padua
San Miguel Arcángel
San Luis Obispo de Tolosa
La Purísima Concepción
Santa Inés Virgen y Mártir
Santa Bárbara
San Buenaventura
Santa Bárbara Presidio
San Fernando Rey de España
San Gabriel Arcángel
Pueblo of Nuestra Señora de Los Ángeles
San Juan Capistrano
San Luis Rey de Francia
San Diego Presidio
San Diego de Alcalá

the long-awaited opportunity to travel to places never visited by other missionaries. As the newly appointed mission president, his job was to establish the missions in Alta California, make sure that each mission had everything that it needed, and oversee the friars who would run each mission.

The Spanish government's first plans were to build a mission in the south (San Diego) and then in the north (Monterey) of Alta California. Another was to be built around the Ventura area. After the first three were established, others would be built in between them along the coast. The road that would eventually connect all twenty-one missions along the coast of Alta California was called *El Camino Real*, or the Royal Road.

FOUNDING THE MISSION

The founding of the mission near Ventura was delayed for twelve years because of disagreements with the governor, Felipe de Neve. Along with about eighty soldiers and their families, Fray Serra finally arrived at the site of the future San Buenaventura mission in 1782. It was located near the Chumash village called Mitsquanaqa'n, which had a population of about 500. Fray Serra founded this ninth mission on March 31. He celebrated Mass that Easter morning before the group raised a large wooden cross to mark the site of the mission. It would be one of six he personally dedicated, and the last mission he would found before his death in 1784.

Fray Serra worked hard in his fifteen years as head of the missions, baptizing more than 6,000 indigenous people. When he died, he was living at Mission San Carlos Borroméo del Río Carmelo, in Carmel, California. Fray Francisco Palóu wrote that mission bells sounded at Serra's passing. Many people mourned the loss of their beloved friar—sailors, soldiers, settlers, priests, and friars, along with more than 600 indigenous people attended his funeral. Today, Fray Junípero Serra is a candidate for sainthood, an honor given by the Catholic Church to someone who has shown an incredible devotion to God.

Fray Serra died in 1784 and was buried at San Carlos Borroméo del Río Carmelo. Today he is a candidate for sainthood, a great honor in the Catholic Church.

5
The Early Days of San Buenaventura

Once the founding ceremony ended, the missionaries were left with a cross in the ground and no mission. Most missions initially had only two priests and five or six soldiers assigned to them—

People still make adobe bricks today.

not enough people to do the work involved in building or maintaining a mission. To get their mission built, the friars needed to attract the nearby Chumash and try to convert them. The missionaries gave food, beads, and trinkets to the Native Americans who helped them with their work, and this often encouraged more to come and work for the Spanish.

Fray Serra left Fray Pedro Benito Cambón in charge of San Buenaventura. The Chumash responded in a positive manner to the Spanish and to Fray Cambón. They helped right away with the building of the chapel for payment, but they resisted joining the life of the community. Those Native Americans who did become Christians and joined the community were called **neophytes**.

BEGINNING TO BUILD MISSION SAN BUENAVENTURA

To gain approval from the viceroys of New Spain, the areas chosen for the missions had to have lots of freshwater for drinking and watering the crops, rich soil that could be used for livestock grazing and farming, and wood for constructing buildings and making tools and furniture.

The Chumash at Mission San Buenaventura constructed a sophisticated irrigation system built from logs and stones that was seven miles (11.3 km) long. Fray Cambón designed the water system, or **aqueduct**, which carried water from the Ventura River to holding tanks behind the mission. About ten years after the mission's founding, engineers from New Spain arrived to show the friars and neophytes how to make the system stronger. Today, the design and construction of this aqueduct from natural materials is recognized as an engineering feat.

The finished aqueduct featured a filtration system for purifying drinking water. It also had reservoirs and valves that controlled the amount of water that flowed into the fields, as well as five separate fountains for drinking and washing. The mission

Much of Mission San Buenaventura was made of adobe bricks, similar to the ones shown above.

MISSION LIFE

While the friars relied on the Chumash to do much of the mission's construction, the Chumash also had other chores.

As in the days before living at the mission, Chumash women were primarily responsible for preparing food, but they had to adapt to the different ingredients and cooking methods introduced by the Spanish. For breakfast, they served *atole*, a type of soup that was made from barley and other grains. Lunch was a dish called *pozole*, a soup made with beans and peas. Atole was also served for supper. The friars also taught the Chumash women how to weave cloth and to make candles, soap, and clothing.

Neophyte men learned leatherwork, wood crafting, and farming. They planted grapes, which were native to the area. Barley, oats, wheat, and oranges, which were all introduced by the Spanish, were also raised at the mission. Over a fifty-year period, the mission

reported producing 191,291 bushels of vegetables and grain.

One of the most profitable industries at Mission San Buenaventura was cattle raising. The meat from cattle was used for food, the fat was used to make candles and soap, and the hides were cured to make leather. Whaling ships anchored near the mission to replenish their food supplies would trade with the friars for cured cattle hides. These hides, called Yankee Dollars, were then transported to the colonies in the East and turned into shoes.

Children also had jobs at the mission. Some helped the women weave baskets or clothing. Others kept birds and animals away from the crops and the wet adobe bricks.

In the morning and again in the afternoon, one friar taught lessons about the Catholic religion to all children over the age of five. After giving morning lessons, the friars toured the mission. They made sure everyone was doing his or her work and that no one had escaped.

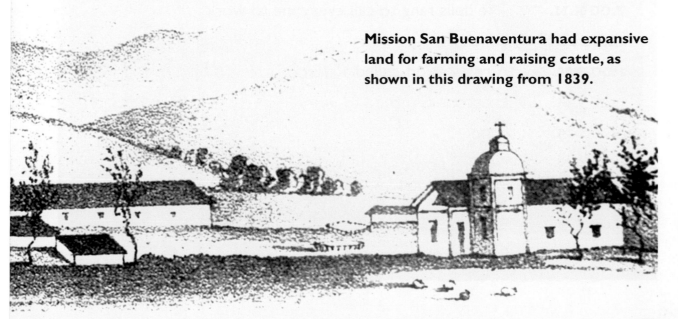

Mission San Buenaventura had expansive land for farming and raising cattle, as shown in this drawing from 1839.

The fountain inside the mission's garden is a unique example of early Spanish architecture and design.

grow a forest of these trees for use as ship masts. The trees were designated California Millennium landmark trees by the America the Beautiful Fund in 2000.

In front of the school stands a life-sized statue of Fray Junípero Serra. You can compare your height to his five-foot, two-inch (1.58 m) frame.

On the other side of the mission is a museum and gift shop. The museum contains artifacts such as vestments worn by the missionaries, the two original wooden bells, baskets woven by Chumash women, and many other objects that were a part of life at Mission San Buenaventura.

In the mission's well-kept gardens, you'll find a running fountain, an old olive press, and a water pump. Two other museums that contain artifacts that are related to Mission San Buenaventura are located nearby. The Albinger Archaeological Museum features pottery and other artifacts dug up in the area, as well as the original foundations of some of the buildings. Right across the street is the Ventura Museum of Natural History, which houses artifacts made by the Chumash.

Mission San Buenaventura is still a vital part of the California landscape—and continues to serve as a link to the rich history of the state of California.

10
Make Your Own Mission Model

To make your own model of Mission San Buenaventura, you will need:

- cardboard
- ruler
- scissors
- tape
- toothpicks
- white and red paint

- sand
- uncooked lasagna noodles
- glue
- moss
- small branches
- small dried flowers

DIRECTIONS

Adult supervision is suggested.

Step 1: Cut a piece of cardboard to measure 24" × 18" (45.7 × 60.9 cm) for your base.

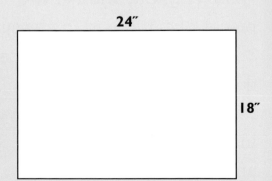

24"

18"

Step 8: To make a bell tower, cut three pieces of cardboard to measure 12" × 3" (30.6 × 7.6 cm). Fold each piece of cardboard every 3" (7.6 cm) into the shape of a box.

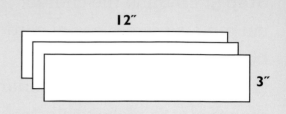

Step 9: Tape the boxes together. This is your bell tower. Tape it to the right inside of your front church wall.

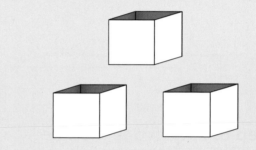

Step 10: Paint the entire mission with white paint mixed with a little sand to give it texture. Let dry.

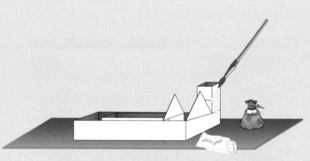

Step 11: Paint the uncooked lasagna noodles with red paint. Let dry.

Step 12: Glue the uncooked lasagna noodles to the tops of your walls.

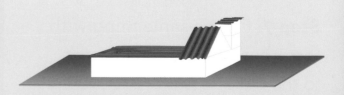

Step 13: Paint a bell on the bell tower and paint windows and doors on the front of the church. Glue two toothpicks together to make a cross.

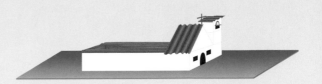

Step 14: Glue moss around the mission to look like grass. Add small branches for trees and small dried flowers.

Use this model as a reference for building your mission.

Glossary

aqueduct (AH-kweh-dukt) A structure such as a pipe or channel that is used to bring water to an area.

baptism (BAP-tih-zum) A sacrament marked by ritual use of water that makes someone a member of a Christian community and cleanses the person of his or her sins.

Christian (KRIS-chun) Someone who follows the Christian religion, or the teachings of Jesus Christ and the Bible.

convert (kun-VURT) To change religious beliefs.

Franciscan (fran-SIS-kin) A member of the Franciscan order, a part of the Catholic Church dedicated to preaching, missionaries, and charities.

friars (FRY-urz) Brothers in a communal religious order. Friars also can be priests.

indigenous people (in-DIJ-en-us PEA-pel) People native born to a particular region or environment.

missionary (MIH-shun-ayr-ee) Someone who is sent to spread his or her religion in another country.

neophyte (NEE-oh-fyt) The name for a Native American once he or she was baptized into the Christian faith.

New Spain (NOO SPAYN) The area where the Spanish colonists had their capital in North America and that would later become Mexico.

parish (PAR-ish) An area with its own church and minister or priest.

petroglyphs (PET-ro-glifs) A carving or inscription on a rock.

presidio (preh-SIH-dee-oh) A Spanish military fort.

quadrangle (KWAH-drang-ul) The square at the center of a mission that is surrounded by four buildings.

reservation (REZ-er-VAY-shun) An area of land in the United States that is kept separate as a place for Native Americans to live.

secularization (seh-kyuh-luh-rih-ZAY-shun) A process by which the mission lands were made to be nonreligious.

viceroy (VYS-roy) A government official who rules an area as a representative of the king.

Pronunciation Guide

Chumash (CHOO-mash)

monjerío (mohn-hay-REE-oh)

pueblo (PWAY-bloh)

ranchería (ran-chuh-REE-ah)

siesta (see-EHS-tah)

temescal (TEH-mes-kal)

tomol (TOH-mul)

tule (TOO-lee)

Find Out More

To learn more about the California missions, check out these books and websites:

BOOKS

Bibby, Brian. *The Fine Art of California Indian Basketry*. Berkeley, CA: Heydey, 2013.

Gibson, Karen Bush. *Native American History for Kids*. Chicago, IL: Chicago Review Press, 2010.

Leffingwell, Randy and Alastair Worden. *California Missions and Presidios*. St. Paul, MN: Voyageur Press, 2005.

Rolle, Andrew and Arthur Verge. *California: A History*. Hoboken, NJ: Wiley-Blackwell, 2007.

Weber, Francis J. *Blessed Fray Junípero Serra: An Outstanding California Hero*. Bowling Green, MO: Editions Du Signe, 2008.

WEBSITES

California Mission Foundation
www.californiamissionfoundation.org
Find quick and easy facts about the missions and discover more about the organization that preserves and protects the missions today.

California Missions Resource Center
www.missionscalifornia.com
Interact with a mission timeline, videos, and photo gallery and unlock key facts about each mission in the California mission system.

Mission San Buenaventura
www.sanbuenaventuramission.org
Discover the history of Mission San Buenaventura and what the mission is like today.

Santa Ynez Chumash
www.santaynezchumash.org
Learn about the last of the recognized tribes of the Chumash at their website.

Index